CANADA'S WOODLAND ANIMALS

Chelsea Donaldson

Scholastic Canada Ltd.

Toronto New York London Auckland Sydney
Mexico City New Delhi Hong Kong Buenos Aires

Scholastic Canada Ltd.
604 King Street West, Toronto, Ontario M5V 1E1, Canada
Scholastic Inc.
557 Broadway, New York, NY 10012, USA
Scholastic Australia Pty Limited
PO Box 579, Gosford, NSW 2250, Australia
Scholastic New Zealand Limited
Private Bag 94407, Greenmount, Auckland, New Zealand
Scholastic Ltd.
Euston House, 24 Eversholt Street, London NW1 1DB, UK

Every reasonable effort has been made to trace the ownership of copyright material used in the book. The publisher would be pleased to know of any errors or omissions.

Visual Credits
Cover, pp. i, iii (border), 5, 6, 14–15: Alan & Sandy Carey/Ivy Images; p. iv: HotHouse Canada; pp. iv–1: Donilo Donadoni/Marka/maxximages.com; pp. 3, 4, 10–13, 17, 19, 34: Thomas Kitchin & Victoria Hurst; p. 7: ©Tom & Pat Leeson/leesonphoto.com; p. 9: IFA-Bilderteam/maxximages.com; p. 16: Maresa Pryor/ AnimalsAnimals/maxximages.com; pp. 18, 24, 26, 27, 36, 37, 42: Bill Ivy/Ivy Images; p. 20: Creatas/maxximages.com; p. 22, 30, 31, 40, 43: © Dwight Kuhn; p. 23: Phyllis Greenberg/AnimalsAnimals/maxximages.com; p. 25: © David Cavagnavo/Visuals Unlimited; p. 28: Corey Hochachka/Design Pics/maxximages.com; p. 29: Breck Kent/AnimalsAnimals/maxximages.com; pp. 32, 35: Wayne Lankinen/Ivy Images; p. 38: Joe McDonald/AnimalsAnimals/maxximages.com; p. 39: © Michael Durham/Minden Pictures; p. 41: Zig Leszczynski/AnimalsAnimals/maxximages.com; p. 44: (top & bottom left) Photodisc via SODA, (bottom right) Jim Clark/U.S. Fish & Wildlife Service via SODA; back cover: Photodisc via SODA

Produced by Focus Strategic Communications Inc.
Project Management and Editorial: Adrianna Edwards
Design and Layout: Lisa Platt
Photo Research: Elizabeth Kelly

Special thanks to Dr. Bill Freedman of Dalhousie University for his expertise.

Library and Archives Canada Cataloguing in Publication
Donaldson, Chelsea, 1959-
Canada's woodland animals / Chelsea Donaldson.
(Canada close up)
ISBN 0-439-94677-8
1. Forest animals—Canada—Juvenile literature.
I. Title. II. Series: Canada close up (Toronto, Ont.)
QL112.D65 2006   j591.73'0971   C2006-900622-9

6 5 4 3 2 1   Printed in Canada   06 07 08 09 10

TABLE OF CONTENTS

Canada's Woodlands

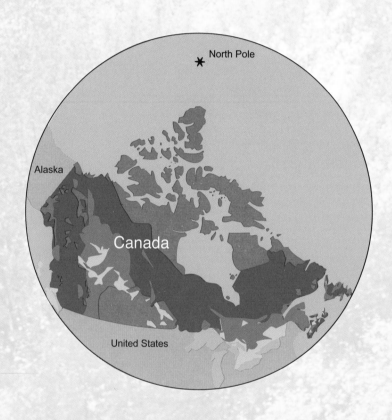

North Pole

Alaska

Canada

United States

■ Evergreen Forest

□ Broad-Leafed Forest

■ Mixed Forest — Evergreen and Broad-Leafed

■ No Forests

Welcome to the Woodlands!

Have you ever wondered why our flag has a maple leaf on it? Perhaps it's because Canada has so many woodlands. Woodlands are areas that are covered in trees.

Canada may be known for its maple trees, but most of its woodlands are made up of evergreen trees, such as pine and spruce. Maples and other broad-leafed trees are found mainly in southern Canada. What kind of woodlands do you have in your part of the country?

Canada's woodlands make wonderful neighbourhoods for wild animals. Each tree is like an animal apartment building. It offers food, shelter and protection to all kinds of woodland creatures. Let's meet some of these forest animals.

CHAPTER ONE

Wolf

A-OOOOOOOOOOO!

There is nothing more haunting than the sound of wolves howling. It can send shivers down your spine.

What do you think wolves are trying to say when they howl? People who study wolves believe they howl to contact other members of their pack. Every wolf has its own particular howl. A pack can stay in contact over long distances by howling. Howling also warns other wolves to stay out of a pack's territory.

A wolf pack is like a family. A wolf may travel far and wide to find food, but it will always return to its pack. Wolves are very loyal.

Every pack has a leader, called the alpha male. He defends the pack's territory by marking the boundaries with his scent.

The leader and his mate are the only members of the pack that have cubs. They also get the best meat from any animal the pack kills. Each wolf in the pack knows who is boss.

Wolves can live almost anywhere there is food available, and woodlands are good hunting grounds. These areas are home to animals such as deer and elk. They are large enough to feed a whole pack.

Wolves often hunt together to take down animals that are much bigger than they are. They creep close to a moose or caribou and try to scare it into running. Then they race alongside and snap at the animal's legs or underbelly until it falls.

Although wolves are fierce hunters, they
are friendly and loving with each other.
All the pack members help to feed and
care for the cubs.

The cubs are born blind, deaf and unable
to walk. But they soon learn to see, hear,
run — and play!

If you know dogs, some wolf behaviours may seem familiar. That's because dogs are related to wolves. For example, both wolves and dogs show they are angry by making their fur stand up and showing their teeth. If they are feeling playful, they dance around and bow with their front paws. Frightened wolves or dogs will flatten their ears right back against their head.

What do you think these young wolves are saying to each other?

CHAPTER TWO

Black Bear

It's springtime in the forest. Small buds are forming on the bare branches of the trees. A pile of melting snow suddenly falls off the high boughs of a pine tree.

In a nearby cave, something rustles and grunts. A minute later, out steps a black bear, just waking up from its long winter sleep. A small black cub follows.

When the cub was born in the winter den, it was about the size of a squirrel. It had no fur, no teeth, a large head and a small back end. Its eyes were still closed. It is hard to believe that one of the largest animals in the woodlands starts out as such a small, helpless creature!

Six weeks after it was born, the cub's eyes
began to open. The cub started to grow fur
and teeth. Now it is three months old.
It must learn how to find its own food.
Both mother and cub are very hungry.

There is not much food around at this time of year. Luckily, bears are not very fussy. They may climb a tree to eat some tender new shoots, or even munch on some pine needles.

As the weather gets warmer, the bears have more food to choose from. Nuts and berries are their favourite snacks. But they also eat insects, mice, rabbits, young moose or deer — and, of course, honey!

Did you know that black bears make a lot of different noises? They can grunt, squeal, huff and even hum or purr. But one thing they don't do is growl.

The cub stays with its mother for the first summer of its life and through the next winter. When the mother is ready to mate again the following spring, she chases the cub away.

The young bear may try several times to come back to its mother. Eventually, it gets the message. Then it sets off to make a life of its own in the woodlands.

CHAPTER THREE

Lynx

Dogs are not the only pets that have wild woodland relatives. Cats have some, too. In fact, a lynx looks a lot like an overgrown house cat. But there are a few differences between a pet cat and a lynx. Can you tell what they are?

For one thing, a lynx has a short, stubby tail. It also has long fur on either side of its face, like a beard, and pointed tufts on its ears.

A lynx has much larger paws than a
domestic cat. In winter, the paws are
covered with thick fur, to act like
snowshoes. They help a lynx walk in
deep snow without sinking down and
getting stuck.

A lynx's light brown or grey fur has white
tips, which look like frost. In summer,
this coat turns reddish brown.

Lynxes live deep in evergreen forests. Sometimes they eat small animals such as mice and birds. Occasionally, they eat larger prey such as deer. But their favourite food by far is the snowshoe hare.

To catch a hare, a lynx hides behind a tree or bush close to a hare's well-used trail. When a hare hops by, the lynx jumps out and grabs it. If the lynx doesn't catch its prey in the first leap, the hare will likely get away. A lynx has excellent eyesight and hearing, but it is not a fast runner.

Lynxes usually hunt alone, but a mother will bring her young along on the hunt when they are old enough. The kittens follow behind their mother in single file, stepping in her tracks. When the lynxes find prey, they spread out and drive the animal until it's trapped between them.

We know very little about lynxes' habits because they usually hunt at night and disappear during the day. These shy cats are very good at hiding. They are one of the most mysterious woodland creatures.

CHAPTER FOUR

White-Tailed Deer

The next time you are walking near a woodland, stay quiet and keep your eyes open. If you are lucky, you may spot a white-tailed deer grazing on some grass near the edge of the forest.

When the deer turns to run, watch closely. It will lift its tail to show a flash of white fur underneath. The white fur is like a flag of warning. It signals to other deer that danger is close by.

White-tailed deer are beautiful creatures. In summer, their fur is reddish brown with patches of white. They have big almond-shaped eyes and long, delicate legs.

A male deer is called a buck. In the spring, two bumps, covered with a soft, velvety fuzz, appear on a buck's forehead. Over the summer, the bumps change. They grow longer and branch outward. At last, in the fall, the velvet dries and peels off, revealing a magnificent set of bone-white antlers.

The antlers may look spectacular, and they may be helpful in finding a mate, but they are not very useful as weapons. Deer have other ways to avoid being eaten by predators.

For one thing, young deer, or fawns, have almost no odour for the first few weeks after they are born. This makes it hard for wolves and other animals to find them. The fawns are also spotted, which helps them blend in with their woodland surroundings. By the time they are three weeks old, they are already fast runners and have excellent eyesight and hearing, just like their parents.

Wolf packs know the places where deer go to feed on grass, buds and fruit. They lie in wait for them. So deer must eat quickly, without really stopping to chew their food. They don't want to become a meal themselves!

Later, when the deer find a safe place, they bring the food back up and chew it properly. This is called "chewing the cud." Deer have four stomachs to help them digest their food this way! What other animals do you know that chew their cud?

CHAPTER FIVE

Skunk

Which woodland animal do you think gets the most respect from its neighbours? No, it's not the fierce wolf or the mighty bear. It's the lowly skunk.

Of course, we all know why skunks are treated so well. When a skunk feels threatened, it uses special glands in its rear end to send out an oily spray that smells *terrible!*

Skunks are peaceful creatures. They spray only if they feel they are in danger. When they do let loose, they lift their tails high, take aim and spray up to five metres — usually right on target!

The spray can blind the unfortunate animal that gets hit by it — but only for a few minutes.

Most animals give a skunk a lot of room to do what it wants. In fact, a skunk often moves right into another animal's burrow instead of digging its own. The family of rabbits or raccoons living there may not be very pleased with the intruder, but they don't dare kick it out.

A skunk eats just about anything it can find. It catches insects, frogs and mice. It also nibbles on fruit, grains and nuts. A skunk that lives near humans often raids the garbage.

In winter, skunks gather in a den. Twelve or more skunks stay together in a tree stump, under a pile of wood or even under the front porch of a house. They don't eat anything during this time. The fat they put on during the summer and fall keeps them alive until spring.

Pregnant females give birth in May or June. They have between four and seven babies, called kits. You can see how small and helpless they look. But don't get too close. Soon the kits will be ready to defend themselves, just like their parents!

CHAPTER SIX

Porcupine

A porcupine is another woodland animal
that has an unusual way to defend itself.
It has over 30,000 sharp needles, or quills,
on its head, back and tail. When a porcupine
feels threatened, it rolls up in a ball. Its quills
stick up like a spiky hairdo. If a curious
animal touches or sniffs the porcupine,
the spikes break off. The intruder is left with
a paw — or a face — full of quills!

It is easy for
the porcupine
to grow more
quills, but it is hard
to take out the ones
it leaves behind.
Porcupine quills are cleverly
designed. They are thin at the tip, so they
break through skin easily. But the tips are
covered in tiny backward-facing barbs, like
fish hooks. So once the quills are inside the
skin, the barbs swell and spread out, making
them very painful to remove. OUCH!

This defence usually works very well.
Although some animals have learned how
to turn a porcupine over to get at its
unprotected belly, most prefer to leave
it alone.

Porcupines are good climbers. Sometimes they sit in the high branches of a tree to feed. With their lumpy, spiky bodies and small eyes, it is easy to mistake them for birds' nests.

Porcupines like to live alone. They may make their dens in the same rock piles as other porcupines, or meet at a favourite feeding ground. But when they do meet, they tend to ignore each other. Although baby porcupines are playful, their parents certainly are not.

Porcupines have orange teeth! In winter, they use their strong teeth to gnaw the inner bark of trees. In summer, they munch on leaves, bushes and grasses.

Because they like to munch on wood, porcupines can create a lot of damage at campsites. They chew on wooden objects, such as axe handles or canoe paddles. This gnawing may help their teeth from getting too long. But it can be very annoying to campers!

CHAPTER SEVEN

Chipmunk

The chipmunk is one of the friendliest creatures in Canada's woodlands. If you place a few nuts or berries near a chipmunk's home and stay very still, you may see the chipmunk dart up to the food, stuff it into its big cheek pouches and then dart away. Eventually, the chipmunk may start to trust you enough to come quite close.

Chipmunks are smaller than their squirrel cousins. While squirrels spend much of their time in trees, chipmunks prefer to stay close to the ground. Their striped coats help them blend in with the streaks of sunlight on the forest floor.

Chipmunks spend the whole summer gathering nuts and seeds for winter. They store the food in wood piles, rock piles or underground in burrows.

A chipmunk's burrow is a long tunnel, about one metre underground.

At one end is a cozy nest area where the chipmunk spends most of the winter, eating its store of food and sleeping.

In spring, females give birth in the nest to three to six baby chipmunks. Only six weeks later, the young chipmunks set out to make their own burrows. This is the most dangerous time for chipmunks.

Until their burrows are finished, they have no easy place to escape from dogs, cats or hawks.

A chipmunk is very clever. To keep its home a secret, it uses a special exit, away from the main entrance, to take dirt out of the tunnel. It carries the earth out in its cheek pouches and spreads it around on the forest floor. That way, predators cannot find any telltale pile of earth near the entrance hole.

Once the digging is done, a chipmunk seals off the work tunnel. It keeps the other entrances well hidden. When winter comes, it stays below ground in the nest — warm, safe and well fed.

CHAPTER EIGHT

Pileated Woodpecker

This is a *pileated* (PIE-lee-ate-ed), or crested, woodpecker. It is perfectly designed for drilling holes in trees. Its beak is flat and thin at the tip and wider near the skull. A rigid tail helps the bird brace itself against a tree trunk. Covered nostrils help keep out sawdust. Under its thick skull is a cushion of air that protects its brain from all the knocking. It's like a power tool with feathers!

Pileated woodpeckers peck wood to find insects burrowed inside. Their long, sticky tongues help them catch and eat the insects. They also drum on posts and trees to mark their territory, attract a mate and communicate with each other.

A woodpecker and its mate choose a tree to nest in. The male woodpecker uses its beak to carve a hole right in the tree. This takes about two weeks of steady pecking.

When the new home is ready, the female lays four to seven eggs. During the day, both parents take turns keeping the eggs warm. At night, the male sits on the eggs while the female sleeps.

Twelve days later, the eggs hatch. Out come tiny, helpless, almost featherless babies.

They grow quickly. After about 18 days, they take turns climbing up and sitting in the hole's opening, looking out at the world. If a bold squirrel or snake tries to get into the hole, it will have to deal with a sharp peck on the head — TOK-TOK-TOK!

CHAPTER NINE

Little Brown Bat

You may think bats are scary creatures. Actually, they aren't scary at all — unless you are a mosquito or a moth.

The most common types of bats in Canada are little brown bats. They really are small. They are only about 4 to 5 centimetres long and 14 centimetres wide with their wings spread out.

Bats have an amazing ability. They can fly quickly through the air, avoiding trees, power lines and houses. They can catch even the tiniest bugs in mid-flight. But what is really amazing is that they can do all this in the dark!

Bats "see" with their ears. They send out high-pitched sound waves that we can't hear. When the sound waves hit a bug or a tree, they bounce back, just as a ball does when it 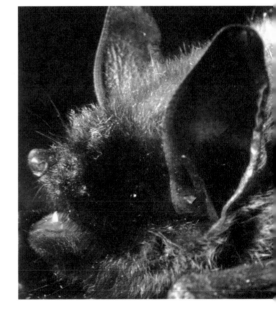 hits a wall. Bats can tell how close the object is by listening to the sound waves. This is called *echolocation* (e-ko-lo-KAY-shun).

Some bats live and hunt on their own. But brown bats live in large groups. During the day, hundreds of them sleep together — in a cave, mine, hollow tree or even the attic of a house. They hold on to perches with their clawed feet and hang upside down. They wrap their wings around themselves for warmth, just like a blanket.

At night, brown bats go out to hunt moths, beetles, mosquitoes and other soft flying insects. A single bat can eat about 600 mosquitoes an hour. Bats are better than bug spray!

You may have heard stories about blood-sucking bats. In South America, vampire bats really do drink blood! But they prefer to feed off cows and other animals, not humans. They don't usually hurt the animals they feed on, either.

And don't worry. None of the bats that live in Canada are interested in your blood!

CHAPTER TEN

Red-Bellied Snake

Canada's woodlands contain many creatures that you hardly ever see. Red-bellied snakes are among these. They are quite common in woodlands, but they usually stay well out of sight during the day. They hide under logs, bushes or piles of leaves.

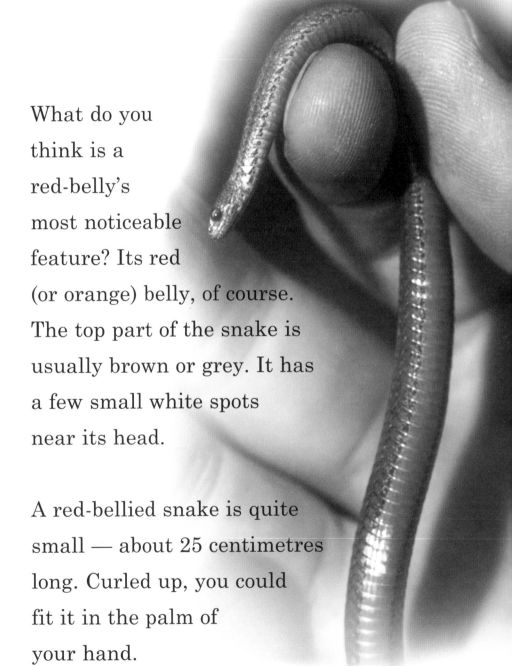

What do you think is a red-belly's most noticeable feature? Its red (or orange) belly, of course. The top part of the snake is usually brown or grey. It has a few small white spots near its head.

A red-bellied snake is quite small — about 25 centimetres long. Curled up, you could fit it in the palm of your hand.

Slugs are red-bellies' favourite food. But these snakes also eat earthworms, snails and even tiny frogs. Red-bellies are so small, they have to watch out for all the animals that find them tasty. Fish, other snakes, chickens, crows, falcons and hawks love to eat red-bellied snakes.

When a red-belly feels threatened, watch out! It flattens its head and body and lets out a smelly fluid. If that doesn't scare away the attacker, the snake may curl its lips into a nasty-looking smile. Perhaps it thinks it looks more terrifying that way. It might also roll around for a while and then "play dead."

A red-bellied snake gives birth to between three and twelve young. The eggs hatch inside the mother, instead of outside. The babies come out one by one. It can take several days for all of them to be born.

In winter, red-bellies hibernate under the ground. This place is called a *hibernaculum* (hy-ber-NACK-you-lum). The snakes often stay together in groups of up to 100. To keep warm, they huddle close together — so close that they form a great big, twisted knot of snake bodies. Imagine what it looks like when they all wake up in the spring and slither away!

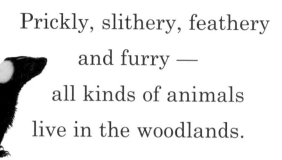

Prickly, slithery, feathery
and furry —
all kinds of animals
live in the woodlands.

Next time you are walking
through a wooded area, keep your
eyes and ears open. You may
just meet some of these
amazing creatures.

Canada's woodlands
are full of surprises!

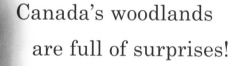